YOUR KNOWLEDGE HAS VALUE

- We will publish your bachelor's and
  master's thesis, essays and papers

- Your own eBook and book -
  sold worldwide in all relevant shops

- Earn money with each sale

Upload your text at www.GRIN.com
and publish for free

Use of CNNs for the Classification of Medical Images

Marwan Al Omari

Bibliographic information published by the German National Library:

The German National Library lists this publication in the National Bibliography; detailed bibliographic data are available on the Internet at http://dnb.dnb.de.

ISBN: 9783346653970
This book is also available as an ebook.

© GRIN Publishing GmbH
Nymphenburger Straße 86
80636 München

Print and binding: Books on Demand GmbH, Norderstedt, Germany
Printed on acid-free paper from responsible sources.

The present work has been carefully prepared. Nevertheless, authors and publishers do not incur liability for the correctness of information, notes, links and advice as well as any printing errors.

GRIN web shop: https://www.grin.com/document/1215084

Running Head: CNNs for Medical Images Classification

Internship in XLIM Laboratory, under the title:

Use of CNNs for the Classification of Medical Images

Submitted by Marwan AL OMARI

This report is addressed for the validation of Master 1 Internship

Master Connected Objects

SP2MI, UFR Fundamental and Applied Sciences

University of Poitiers

Internship Period: 26 April, 2021 - 26 June, 2021

Academic year

2020 - 2021

CNNs for Medical Images Classification

Table of Contents

List of Figures

List of Tables

Acknowledgments

I would like to send my sincere regards and thanks to Mme. Olfa Ben Ahmed who has been supervising me during the internship, on the research project for classifying the medical images. Therefore, I was able to succussed in applying transfer learning into the architecture of VGG16. It is worth to mention the great help, encouragement, guidance, and support I received from her all the time.

Moreover, I wish to express my thanks and gratitude to Coursera's learning platform because it always gives me the opportunity to explore further knowledge, which is beyond my physical boundaries. Also, I would like to thank my brothers and my mother for the constant support and encouragement I have received throughout my journey. As well as, I would like to thank all the equip of the master intelligent objects especially M. Clency Perrine and M. Noël Richard for their constant efforts in helping out students in achieving their studies at the university of Poitiers.

CNNs for Medical Images Classification

Abstract (English)

Deep learning models have showed great capabilities in data modelling on the various applications of image processing, including segmentation, classification, tagging, and many others. In particular, convolutional neural network (CNNs) has proved to be effective in capturing deep features on unstructured data that are well sited in the state-of-the-art. It is well competitive in comparison to the traditional algorithms of machine learning. This research project, therefore, structures different enhanced architectures and models of CNNs using in particular the VGG16 model, for its featured simplicity and efficiency along with its pre-trained wights on ImageNet. The VGG16 models are well trained using transfer learning mechanism in fine-tuning the architecture on the ISIC2018 Task3 dataset. Then, the models are projected for skin cancer image classification in highlighting the state-of-the-art performance. The four proposed architectures of VGG16 have achieved real competitive results on four different and unique environments. They are well manifest in employing different fine-tuning and freezing layers techniques. In experiments, the VGG16 FU, which by all the layers of VGG16 fine-tuned on the dataset, achieved a total accuracy of 0.903 accuracy and 0.896 loss in validation data, and 0.904 accuracy and 0.893 loss in test data

Keywords: Convolutional Neural Network (CNN), Image Processing, Image Classification, Deep Learning (DL).

Abstract (Résumé en Français)

Les modèles d'apprentissage profond (deep learning) ont montré de grandes capacités dans la modélisation des données pour diverses applications de traitement d'images, notamment la segmentation, la classification, l'étiquetage et bien d'autres. En particulier, les réseaux de neurones convolutifs (CNN) se sont avérés efficaces pour capturer des caractéristiques profondes sur des données non structurées, ce qui se traduit par des performances de pointe par rapport aux algorithmes traditionnels d'apprentissage automatique (machine learning). Ce projet de recherche structure donc différentes architectures et modèles améliorés de CNNs en utilisant en particulier VGG16 pour la simplicité et l'efficacité de ses caractéristiques ainsi que ses poids pré-entraînés sur ImageNet. Les modèles sont bien formés en utilisant le mécanisme d'apprentissage par transfert pour affiner les modèles VGG16 sur le jeu de données ISIC2018 Task3. Les modèles sont projetés pour la classification d'images de cancer de la peau en mettant en évidence les performances de l'état de l'art. Les quatre architectures proposées de VGG16 ont obtenu des résultats compétitifs sur quatre environnements différents et uniques en employant différentes techniques de fine-tuning et freezing layers. Dans les expériences, le VGG16 FU, qui par toutes les couches du VGG16 affiné sur le jeu de données, a atteint une précision totale de 0,903 précision et 0,896 perte dans les données de validation, et 0,904 précision et 0,893 perte dans les données d'essai

Mots-clés : Réseau de neurones convolutif (CNN), traitement d'images, classification d'images, apprentissage profond (DL).

XLIM Laboratory and Internship Presentations

The internship opportunity I had with XLIM laboratory was a great chance to further my learning and professional careers in image processing and deep learning (DL). Thus, I do consider myself as lucky individual for the having the right position in data and machine learning (ML) engineering. I am so grateful for having the chance to discover many grateful resources of knowledge and skills of independency, research, and development. I am with great confidence I could say I am lucky to meeting different specialists in DL and ML. In general, they have led me of course to the right and better place through the internship period from April 26 to June 26 in the year 2021.

XLIM is one of the French research centers they are known under the name of CNRS (Centre national de la recherche scientifique) [21]. It is numbered as 7252, which is greatly centered on electronics, optics, photonics, mathematics, computer science, image processing, telecommunication, network security, bio-engineering, and energy. XLIM is a multidisciplinary research institute, located on several geographical sites, in Limoges on the sites of the Faculty of Science and Technology, the ENSIL, Ester-Technopole, on the University Campus of Brive and in Poitiers on the site of the Futuroscope Technopole. It brings together more than 440 teacher-researchers, CNRS researchers, engineers, technicians, post-doctoral and doctoral students, and administrative staff. Its research work is based on two platforms.

On one hand, a platform gives researchers access to technological equipment for the creation of optical structures, for instance, large pool of lasers and instruments for the experimental characterization of electronic, optical, electromagnetic and radiating devices. On the other hand, the laboratory engaged in modeling and simulation activities. It is equipped with a software forge which is available to XLIM members and their external collaborators, as it offers multiscale simulation of complex systems based on models at the interface between physics, mathematics and computer science.

During my internship training, I have been an essential engineer to develop and experiment DL architectures for solving the problem of medical image classification. I have learned many information that will be my next source for knowledge-making and strategy development. I was responsible at first to discover the whole functioning of the ISIC challenge in medical context aside from the complexity of its data. Then, I have had the position to analyze the dataset in much deeper manipulations in using programming languages, for example, python manipulated in *Jupyter Notebook*. I looked to the data with critical view with the help of data visualization for further predicating the future-base solutions. Afterward, I could develop the whole architecture of DL to classify the 7 classes of images, using much transfer learning along with deeper network of DL. Therefore, I have had to identify the state-of-the-art solutions and algorithms for better the results, including pre-processing methods and algorithms structures. I have tested and experimented much DL algorithms for fine-tuning the CNNs algorithm that I had developed for the task 3 of classification on ISIC2018 dataset. Examples of these algorithms are LeNet and VGG16. At the final stages of learning, I had adopted VGG16 architecture for the image classification that I had incorporated into four different settings of experience and evaluations.

During visual meetings, I had to present the results that I came up in each step with clear presentation; so, through presentations, my native English as well as French languages were improving in oral and written communications as I was writing weekly reports and emails to my supervisor.

In addition to the technical tasks, my skills, as a part of XLIM's Internship program in image processing, been developed massively in communication, organization, independent research, analytical vision, curiosity, and creativity. I have learnt to present ideas with good communication skills in both verbal and written forms. The writing is not free of limitations though I have tried my best to keep the writings free from errors.

As for importance, I have found organization an essential part for time management and task handling as I was reasonable for different tasks in every step of advancement. Data science and DL require dynamic and analytical mind in visualizing fitted-solution after recovering a wide literature background in related work in image classification. The literature review has enabled me in identifying problems at each time I make an advancement in the development of the DL architecture as a whole.

In daily bases, I was learning new things that had shaped my mind in data science and artificial intelligence (AI). I believe I have proved myself as an essential member in providing revolutionary ideas and innovative solutions to improve image classicization through transfer learning. However, I have faced many problems in setting up the environment for training the algorithms as I could not benefit from the materials and supports of the XLIM laboratory in training the algorithms as well as furthering into the state-of-the-art improvements. I have been truly limited in my personal computer, which it was crashing in learning with huge amount of data in complicated settings.

In sum, I have really obtained great insights into the key performance and potential capacity of image processing methodologies through data analysis and algorithmic development. I believe they are rarely manifested in French research laboratories especially during the difficult time of Covid-19 pandemic.

1. Introduction

Image processing employs different and multiple methodologies from hand-forged features to machine learning (ML) for the objectives of detection, classification, and segmentation. Here as a recent development in ML, deep learning (DL) employs deeper processing units called neurons to learn hierarchical features and representations of data [23]. DL outperforms humans' predictions as it is well going into impressive advancement and evolvement in the different fields of science as in computer vision [14]. The classification of images generalized to the concern of DL in distinguishing their different classes and categories. Therefore, DL architectures specialized with CNNs could harness features of different levels according to its different layers order, algorithm deepness or complexity, and data size [12]. Therefore, as a solution, with fine-tuning, DL could use transfer learning (TL) as a matter of fact in reusing other architecture of DL that was pre-trained on datasets to current problems between hands. This technique has proved a promising result that is well competitive to humans [20].

In the context of medical images, it is the same case with fine-tuning in the proposition and classification tasks. As it is well proved, CNNs achieve competitive results in performance with experts of skin cancer [20]. As for the aim of this internship, we have, therefore, adopted pre-trained VGG16 model on ImageNet for the ISIC2018 task 3 datasets because it is easier to fine-tuning its layers. The data is in widely used for the improvements of benign and malignant skin lesions diagnosis. It contains 10015 training dermatoscopic images collected over 20 years from two different countries, Austria and Australia. There are a total of seven lesions types, which we would discover later on.

The works of this projects are specified in 5 sections. The first section is already introduced the subject under study. Later in the second section, we would discover the related works that are well provided towards the image classification of ISIC2018 challenge. The section 3 would detail the DL background in the context of medical diagnosis along with the ISIC2018 dataset. The fourth section would specify the approach in discussing the pre-processing steps, algorithms, and evaluation metrices. The fifth section, we would present the results of the experiments with dedicated analysis. The sixth section would conclude the whole idea of the research project in highlighting the challenges along with further improvements to be make. Lastly, there would be the numbered references to be easily researched through.

2. Related Work

In this section, we would present the main research articles that worked on ISIC challenges for the aim of better understanding the literature and the employed techniques in their approaches in respect with our project study. At the end of this section, we would provide a briefing of the studies in a form of a briefed table.

[10] The writer worked on classifying 25331 images of ISIC2019 Task 1 dataset for 8 classes of skin lesions, including melanoma (MEL), melanocytic nevus (MV), basal cell carcinoma (BCC), actinic keratosis (AK), benign keratosis (BKL), dermatofibroma (DF), Squamous cell carcinoma (SCC) and vascular lesion (VASC). He proceeded with preprocessing the images to 600x450 pixels, then applied color constancy [5] to eliminate the variance of luminance and color. Afterwards, the pixels of images are normalized to values between 0 and 1. Next, data are augmented with cropping and random flipping. Therefore, the resulting pictures were cropped by 224x224 pixels. Their model was configured in Google Colab through manipulating the hyperparameters in specifying the learning rate (LR) of Adam optimizer at 0.0001 (reduced

by 0.5 after 2 epochs) and the choice of early stopping through using checkpoint at the top validation accuracy (ACC). The researcher has made use of weighted loss function, which would punish the wrong predictions of classes with lower samples. Data split into 80% training and 20% validation set. In retraining the DenseNet model, it had achieved 91% ACC but with low recall of MEL due to its similarity to NV class. As a consequence, he enhanced the architecture by using an ensemble model of DenseNet and Inception, achieving 88% ACC, through averaging their results in weighted loss function to punish false negatives for MEL and increase recall in decreasing precision. He declared that having false positive is lesser dangerous than false negatives. Also, the fine-tuning of the model on ImageNet dataset has performed better than a model that training a model from the scratch. As for future propositions, he would use the state-of-the-art of convolutional neural networks (CNNs) such as applying Squeeze-and-Excitation [7], Residual Neural Networks [18], and changing the loss function to focal loss [6] for reducing the harm of the unbalance data. However, he declared many problems in his research, including: the unavailability of graphics processing units (GPUs). He had noted that the dataset is imbalanced like the previous dataset of ISIC2018, especially for Dermatofibroma and Vascular Lesions. This problem goes back to extraction of data from different sources.

[8] They proposed a deep convolutional neural networks (CNNs) architecture based on DenseNet with a high discriminating learning methodology employed by using center-loss function for the classification of ISIC2019 Task 1 skin lesions: MEL, MV, BCC, AK (Bowen's disease), BKL, DF, and VASC lesion. Their model composed in Caffe framework of total 61 layers DenseNet-121 on 224 × 224 input images. They modified each dense blocks from 4 to 3, where the third layer composed of 22 convolutional layers instead of 48 ones. Between two dense blocks, they used 1x1 convolution followed by 2x2 average pooling. At the last block before the final output layer, a global average pooling (pool5) is performed. The model pretrained on ImageNet dataset, which is fine-tuned on ISIC 2018 third task. In the training phase, a linear combination of soft-max and center-loss functions are employed as total loss function. For each class, 80% of images considered for training and the remaining 20% for validation. A further subdivision was created so there are no common pictures between the training and validation sets for every category of pictures. Data augmented through geometric transformations such as rotations and flipping. As a result, the resulting patch was resized to the dimension of network input layer (224×224 pixels). Stochastic gradient descent (SGD) was used for optimization with LR starting at 0.01, weight decay and momentum equal to 0.0001 and 0.9 respectively. The maximum number of iterations has been set at 75000, decreasing the LR by a factor of 10 at each step of 20000 iterations. The proposed system performed an overall score of 89.2 % in the validation phase. Finally, they proposed further pre-processing steps such as the use of segmentation to obtain registered images into a common reference.

[9] They experimented various neural networks like PNASNet-5-Large, InceptionResNetV2, SENet154, InceptionV4, and an ensemble of all previous models. ISIC2018 task 3 and HAM 1000 data pre-processed through normalizing and subtracting mean RGB value of ImageNet, conversion of pixels to range from 0 to 1, and resizing their dimensional size to X. Also, the researcher augmented the number of images by rotation, flipping, random cropping, adjust brightness and contrast, pixel jittering, Aspect Ratio, random shearing, zooming, and vertical and horizontal shifting. These different representations would extract extra features out of fed images for better differentiation and classification. For fine-tuning, the experimenter used pre-trained ImageNet model to initialize the network and freeze some layers for some iterations and

then unfreeze them to avoid unstable gradient flow. He used early stopping and Adam optimization at 0.01 LR, as well as cross-entropy loss function for changing the weights by back-propagation. He achieved a validation score of 0.76 for PNASNet-5-Large, 0.70 for InceptionResNetV2, 0.74 for SENet154, 0.67 for InceptionV4, and 0.73 for the Ensemble one. As a conclusion, the ensemble model has achieved competitive classification performance in contrast to single models. However, the researcher has found many difficulties, including the unbalanced dataset with large differences in the distribution of images' classes. Finally, he proposed adding and using a future bigger dataset with improved feature variety, adding additional regularization tweaks, and fine-tuning of hyper-parameters

[11] They explored the effect of input images' sizes ranging from 64x64 to 768x768 on the classification performance of fine-tuned CNNs, namely DenseNet-121, ResNet-18, and ResNet-50. Input sizes include 5 types: 64 × 64, 128 × 128, 224×224, 448×448, and 768×768 pixels. They used ISIC2016 and ISIC2017 datasets, which include three types of skin lesions (MM, SK, BN). The researcher considered 2184 images for training and 600 images for validation after they have augmented them using rotations and flipping techniques. Hence after, they pre-processed the data by applying grayworld color constancy [5] that is well normalizing the colors of images. Secondly, they subtracted the mean intensity RGB value of ImageNet dataset as well as resized the images to the proposed five resolutions using bicubic interpolation and aspect ratio for non-squared images. The manufactured model has replaced the fully connected layers (FCL) of pre-trained networks by new FCL with 3 nodes to match the three types of skin lesions. In addition, the cells' weights were randomly initialized from Gaussian distribution. The same technique used in [9] in freezing the layers while training the network, it was well used to avoid overfitting. The mode tested on three different optimizers: stochastic gradient descent (SGD) of LR 0.9 with momentum of LR 0.001 (SGDM), root mean square propagation (RMSProp) of LR 0.0001, and adaptive moment estimation (Adam) of LR 0.0001. The batch size varies from 6 to 64 images for 15 epochs. Their approach based on building blocks of training with 108 sub-models and one-versus-all methodology, as in feeding each 4 models with different resolutions and then taking their average outputs for each corresponding class. Their algorithm implemented in MatLab (ver. 2018a) based on the MatConvNet framework and the MatLab Neural. The computation specifications are: Intel Corei5-6600k 3.50 GHz CPU, 16 GB of RAM and a single Nvidia GTX 1070 card with 8 GB of installed memory Network Toolbox. In experiment, the average results are 89.31%, 89.41%, 90.81% and 91.44% for input image resolutions of 128 × 128, 224 × 224, 448 × 448 and 768 × 768 pixels, respectively. On the other hand, in the fusion method, they obtained an improved average area under the curve (AUC) values of 90.32%, 90.64%, 92.52% and 92.52% for ResNet-18, ResNet-50, and DenseNet-121, respectively. Finally considering the average performance of each model for various image resolutions, the results are 90.93%, 90.11% and 89.68%, respectively. As a conclusion, the researchers remarked a higher performance on larger image sizes, whereas the problem has persisted in downsampling, which is leading to a loss of useful medical information.

[12] They have contributed to the literature with novel data augmentation strategy in 16 multi-crop strategies with averaging their predicted values as the final prediction, combination of DropOut and DropBlock regularizations to reduce overfitting and RandAugment. Term RandAugment proposed to address the defects of sample underrepresentation in the HAM dataset, which it would greatly reduce the search space and thereby shorten the training time

and the computational cost as well. Also, they had integrated Novel multi-weighted focal loss function and class-balanced loss as a solution to overcome the uneven sample size, more especially, in the scenario where the skin lesions have low contrast, fuzzy borders and interferences such as hair, veins or ruler marks. The RandAugment consists of 14 search space available transformations. For transformation of each image, a parameter-free procedure is applied in order to reduce the parameter space while maintaining the image diversity. RandAugment (randomly selected for color and shape transformations) comprises 2 integer hyperparameters N and M, where N is the number of transformations applied to the training images, and M is the magnitude of each augmentation distortion. A randomly selected transformation is applied to each image accordingly to the preset magnitude, followed by repetition of process N-1 times. All the transformations use the same global parameter M so that the search space size is significantly reduced from 10^{32} to 10^2. They tested various Deep CNNs (DCNNs) from classical VGG series to RegNet series but finally adapted RegNetY-32GF, which are all measured in balanced ACC (BACC). Their models are initialized with the pre-trained weights on the ImageNet dataset, and fine-tuned on the HAM training set of batch size of 128. The experiments launched on 2 NVIDIA GeForce GTX 2080Ti graphics cards using PyTorch platform. Adam and MultiStepLR optimizers with LR of 0.001 reduced to 0.1 per epoch from total 30th epochs where early stopping is used after 70 epochs. RegNetY-3.2G achieves a best of 0.858 BACC, which is 0.005 higher than the best result of EfficientNet-b2. Finally, the results achieved for general augmentation method of 0.831, RandAugment of 0.850, Modified RandAugment of 0.860 BACC.

[12] Their study achieves a high classification performance at a low cost of computational resources. Their model is well of great potential for working on mobile devices for automated screening of skin lesions as well as developing automatic diagnosis tools in other clinical disciplines. They had declared that most of the accessible datasets for skin lesions do not have a sufficient sample size and the problem is that increasing the overall capacity may induce transition of the models from an under-fitting to an over-fitting area.

Table 1- Articles Summarization in respect to study number, dataset, used approach, results, challenges and the possible future works

Study	Dataset	Approach	Results	Problems and Challenges	Future work
[10]	**Description:** ISIC2019 Task 1 dataset of 25331 images for 8 classes of skin lesions. **Pre-processing:** - Reshaping images to 600x450 pixels - Color constancy - Pixel normalization to values 0 and 1 - Data augmentation with cropping and random flipping - Image cropping 224x224 pixels **Training set:** 80% of the dataset **Validation set:** 20% of the dataset	**Platform:** Google Colab **Configuration:** - 0.0001 Learning rate (LR) adaptive moment estimation (Adam) (reduced by 0.5 after 2 epochs) - Early stopping - Weighted loss function - Pretrained on ImageNet **Models:** - Single model of DenseNet - Ensemble model of DenseNet and Inception	**ACC:** - Single model is 91% - Ensemble model is 88%	- Unavailability of GPUs - Imbalanced both datasets ISIC2018 and ISIC2019	Including: - Squeeze-and-Excitation - Residual Neural Networks - Focal loss function

CNNs for Medical Images Classification

Study	Dataset	Approach	Results	Problems and Challenges	Future work
[8]	**Description:** ISIC2019 Task 1 dataset of 25331 images for 8 classes of skin lesions. **Pre-processing:** - Reshaping input images to 224 × 224 pixels - Data augmentation with geometric transformations such as rotations and flipping **Training set:** 80% of the dataset **Validation set:** 20% of the dataset	**Platform:** Caffe framework **Configuration:** - Center-loss function - Soft-max function - Pretrained on ImageNet - Stochastic gradient descent (SGD) of 0.01 LR - 0.0001 weight decay - 0.9 momentum - 75000 iterations number - Decreasing LR by factor 10 each 20000 iterations **Models:** - DenseNet-121, includes: - 61 layers - 22 convolutional layers (1x1) - Average pooling (2x2) - 3 dense block number	ACC: - 89.2 %	- Unbalance dataset - Increase CNNs performance	Further data pre-processing: - Segmentation
[9]	**Data:** - ISIC2018 Task 3 dataset of 10015 training and 193 validation images for 7 classes of skin lesions. - HAM 1000 (HAM) **Pre-processing:** - Image normalization in subtracting mean RGB value of ImageNet - Pixel normalization to values 0 and 1 - Reshaping input images to 224 × 224 pixels - Data augmentation with otation, flip, random crop, adjust brightness, adjust contrast, pixel jitter, Aspect Ratio, random shear, zoom, and vertical and horizontal shift **Training set:** - 10015 images - Images from HAM 1000 (number not specified) **Validation set:** 193 images	**Platform:** Pytorch **Configuration:** - Models Pretrained on ImageNet - Using the technique of layers freezing and unfreezing - 0.01 LR Adam - Cross-entropy loss function -Early stopping **Models:** - PNASNet-5-Large - InceptionResNetV2 - SENet154 - InceptionV4 - Ensemble model of all previous models	ACC: - PNASNet-5-Large is 76% - InceptionResNetV2 is 70% - SENet154 is 74% - InceptionV4 is 67% - Ensemble model is 73%	- Unbalanced dataset - High time consumption of training and fine-tune procedures	Including: - Future bigger dataset - Improved feature variety - Regularization tweaks - Hyper-parameters fine-tuning
[11]	**Description:** Both datasets include three types of skin lesions (MM, SK, BN)	**Platform:** MatLab (ver. 2018a) - MatConvNet framework	**Average area under the curve (AUC):**	- Downsampling - Computational	Further experiments with:

5

CNNs for Medical Images Classification

Study	Dataset	Approach	Results	Problems and Challenges	Future work
	- ISIC2016 - ISIC2017 **Pre-processing:** - Data augmentation with geometric transformations such as rotations and flipping - Grayworld color constancy 5 pixels modes of - Image normalization in subtracting mean RGB value of ImageNet - Reshaping input images to 5 modes: 64 × 64, 128 × 128, 224×224, 448×448, and 768×768, using bicubic interpolation and aspect ratio for non-squared images **Training set:** 2184 images **Validation set:** 600 images	- MatLab Neural **Configuration:** - Fully Connected layers with 3 nodes - Random weight initialization - 0.9 LR SGD - 0.001 LR SGD momentum (SGDM) - 0.0001 LR root mean square propagation (RMSProp) - 0.0001 LR Adam - Variation of batch size from 6 to 64 images - 108 sub-models - One-versus-all methodology **Models:** - DenseNet-121 - ResNet-18 - ResNet-50 - Ensemble model of all averaging results of the previous models	- DenseNet-121 is 89.68% - ResNet-18 is 90.93% - ResNet-50 is 90.11% - Ensemble model is 91.5%	Limitations - Ensemble model is not suitable for clinical settings because of model derivation	- Images larger than 768 × 768
[12]	**Description:** HAM 1000 (HAM) is one of the biggest dermoscopic image datasets, contains solely 10015 pictures, which is the same as ISIC2018 dataset **Pre-processing:** - RandAugment (14 search space transformations) **Training set:** 10015 images **Validation set:** 193 images	**Platform:** PyTorch **Configuration:** Regularizations: - DropOut - DropBlock - Multi-weighted Focal Loss function - Class-balanced loss function - Batch size of 128 images - Pretrained on ImageNet - Early stopping Optimizers: - 0.001 LR Adam - 0.001 MultiStepLR **Models:** - RegNetY-3.2G - EfficientNet-b2	**Balanced ACC (BACC):** - RegNetY-3.2G is 85.8% - EfficientNet-b2 is 85.3% **Modes:** - General augmentation is 83.1% - RandAugment is 85.0% - Modified RandAugment is 86.0%	- Low sample size - Transition from under-fitting to over-fitting	Not specified

3. Background

In this section, we would discuss the DL in the context of medical diagnosis in highlighting the CNNs architectures and transfer learning, as well as detailed description of ISIC2018 dataset.

3.1 Deep Learning in Medical Diagnosis

Artificial intelligence (AI) and machine learning (ML) are the hope in changing the medical diagnosis situation in avoiding acknowledged mistakes and harmful medical errors. They would better the diagnosis of symptoms, which are tricky to spot even by best experts.

Deep learning (DL), as a one part of the broader family of ML methods, based on artificial neural networks (ANNs) with representation learning in reinforcement, supervised, semi-supervised, and unsupervised methods [15]. DL architectures such as deep neural networks (DNNs), recurrent neural networks (RNNs) and convolutional neural networks (CNNs) have been applied to fields including computer vision, natural language processing (NLP), machine translation (MT), and medical image analysis, where they have produced competitive results that would surpass human's performance.

In general, Artificial neural networks (ANNs) were inspired by information processing and distributed communication nodes in biological systems. ANNs have various differences from biological brains in the tendance to be static and symbolic, while the biological brain tends to be dynamic and analogue. However, the main core of deep learning refers to the use of multiple layers to progressively extract higher-level features from a raw input. For example, in image processing, lower layers may identify edges, while higher layers may identify the concepts relevant to a human such as digits or letters or faces.

Nowadays, DL remains the most promising and widely used ML technique for radiology in particular and disease detection in general. It comes as no surprise as diagnostic imaging prevails in clinical diagnosis and image recognition. In 2016, Geoffrey Hinton, a notable computer scientist and researcher, predicted that radiologists and specialists who diagnose diseases from medical imaging like X-rays, computed tomography (CT) scans, and magnetic resonance imaging (MRI); they would soon lose their jobs. "People should stop training radiologists right now," he announced, "It's obvious that within five years deep learning is going to do better than humans," [14].

It is clear that the advancement of DL makes it much useful but not much reliable to the level that Hinton indicted by which machines would replace human experts. However, DL is still used to support the doctors in pre-selection and prioritize cases, but not as a main tool to diagnose patients.

From here, there are diverse use of DL in radiology and other diagnostic practices:

1. Detecting the Neurological Abnormalities
2. Screening of the Common Cancers
3. Identifying the Infections in Kidney & Liver
4. Brain Tumor Detection with High Accuracy
5. Dental Imaging Analysis
6. Detecting the Bone Fractures and Musculoskeletal Injuries

3.2 Deep Learning architectures
DL architectures are plain after the celebrated victory of AlexNet [17] at the LSVRC2012 classification contest. Also, the deep Residual Network (ResNet) [18] is arguably a groundbreaking research in the computer vision in the last few years. However, all these developed architectures are based on the CNN algorithm. In this section, we would give much details concerning CNNs in taking LeNet-5, published by Yann LeCun in 1998 [23] architecture, as an example of illustration,

3.3 Convolutional Neural Networks (CNNs)
CNNs or ConvNets is commonly used in computer vision in tasks of classification, detection, and also regression.

CNNs for Medical Images Classification

In general, the CNNs take an input as an array, for example, an image, would be based on an array of pixels and would depend on its resolution. The proposed input would be in shape of height (h) x width (w) x dimension (d). The d could refer to RGB by indicator 3 and 1 for grayscale images. To proceed into training and testing CNNs model, each input image pass through series of convolution layers with specified filters (kernels), pooling, fully connected layers (FCL), and loss functions for final probabilistic classification. As for clear explanation of CNNs, LeNet-5, as it is well visualized in figure (1), would be used to demonstrate the different layers of CNNs.

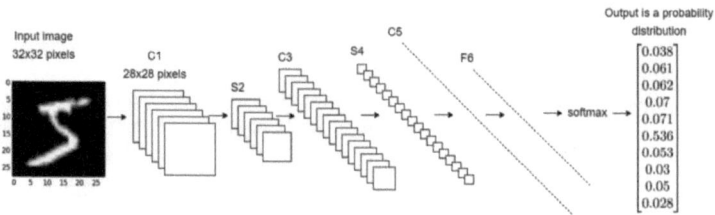

Figure 1- LeNet-5, an example of CNNs architecture, which extracted from [19]

3.3.1 Convolution Layer (C1, C3, and C5)
The first layer that would extract features from the input image in preserving the relationship between pixels by learning image features using small squares of data. It uses a mathematical operation of two inputs as like image matrix and a kernel. Such filters include, for example, edge detection, blur, and sharpen. The filter makes use of stride, which is the number of pixels shifts over the input data. So, if the stride is set to 4, the filter would move 4 pixels at a time and so forth.

3.3.2 Pooling Layer (S2 and S4)
Downsampling or subsampling works in reducing the number of parameters when the input images are large. There are different types of pooling, as follows:

- Max Pooling takes the largest element from the feature map.

- Average Pooling takes the average element from the feature map.

- Sum Pooling takes the sum of all elements from the feature map.

3.3.3 FCL (F6)
The image matrix flattened into vector to be fed into FCL through ANNs, where an activation function, as for instance, softmax function would be there to classify the outputs of fed images.

3.4 Transfer Learning (TL)
There are many limitations of DL to generate a good result in comparison to the environment it was applied on. So, the DL models still disadvantage in capabilities to be generalized on unseen clinical data. This problem goes back most often to the limited number of training data. Therefore, the only solution here is to find more data. However, it is much difficult to find available datasets without paying much money or it is just restricted to a group of people. Transfer learning (TL) makes it possible because of the similar distribution of colors between images to use available pretrained models, on other datasets as like imageNet, on fine-tuning a new DL model.

As a concept, TL pretrains a model on different task from the original one and then saving the learned weights to be later used on, for initializing the parameters of the model in fine-tuning with the desired dataset for the objective task. In addition, to understand TL much more in the context of medical imaging, Raghu et al. provided significant remarkable guidelines for researchers [20]. Most importantly, TL has proven to enhance general performance in the usage of large and deep model such as ResNet and InceptionNet. These models change less during fine-tuning for they had extracted different features in pretraining phase. However, initializing a random weight would limit the model to create significant features from input images.

In addition, transferring scale range of the weights through their mean and variance from the pretrained phase instead of the weights themselves facilitate model's convergence. Hence, initializing the layers with inherited scaling of the pretrained weights rather than the weights would reduce the complexity of the model as well as the computation time for finding the function's optimum. As we could see it is well manifested in figure (2)

Moreover, inheriting the pretrained weight for the first two layers of the fine-tuning model would have an impact over its convergence because of the concentration of meaningful features in the first few layers.

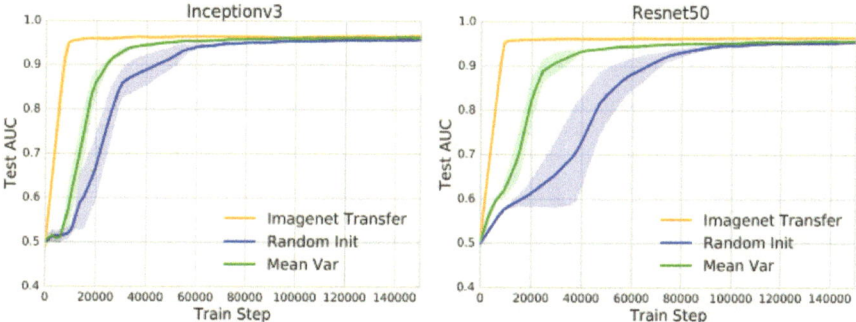

Figure 2- The effect of ImageNet pretraining on the convergence of the model, extracted from [20]

3.5 ISIC Dataset
ISIC stands for international skin imaging collaboration; it has three tasks:

- Task 1- Lesion Segmentation.
- Task 2- Lesion Attribute Detection.
- Task 3- Disease Classification.

Our main goal is Task 3 that directed to the prediction of skin diseases within the dermoscopic images. It includes 7 classes as specified in table (2): Melanoma, Melanocytic nevus, Basal cell carcinoma, Actinic keratosis / Bowen's disease (intraepithelial carcinoma), Benign keratosis (solar lentigo / seborrheic keratosis / lichen planus-like keratosis), Dermatofibroma, Vascular lesion [4].

MEL	NV	BCC	AKIEC	BKL	DF	VASC	Total
1113	6705	514	327	1099	115	142	10015

Table 2- ISIC2018 Task 3 training dataset, number of images for each class

In the training set, there are a total of 10015 skin lesion images from 7 skin diseases: Melanoma (1113), Melanocytic nevus (6705), Basal cell carcinoma (514), Actinic keratosis (327), Benign keratosis (1099), Dermatofibroma (115) and Vascular (142).

On the other hand, the validation dataset consists of 193 images. Figure (3) shows image examples of these 7 types of the skin lesions.

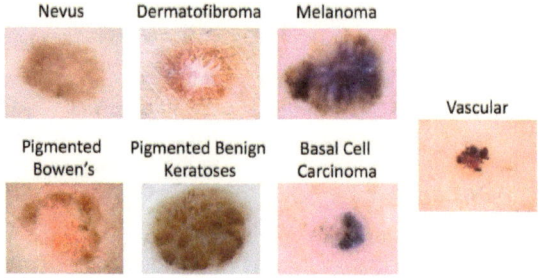

Figure 3- Image examples of ISIC2018 Task 3, extracted from [4]

However, the test data that is noy provided in the challenge, there are well the photos provided but there is no possibility of accessing their labels though I have tried to participate in the ISIC2018 challenge. They have requested a manuscript for the project along with data files in .csv, which is totally out understanding. So, I had used a 25% of the training set for testing the 4 CNNs models.

2018

Task	Training Data	Training Ground Truth	Validation Data	Validation Ground Truth	Test Data	Test Ground Truth	License
1		Download (28MB)		Download (742KB)		Not Available ⑦	
	Download (10.4GB) 2594 images and 12870 corresponding ground truth response masks (5 for each image).		Download (228MB)		Download (2.2GB) 1000 images.		CC-0
2		Download (33MB)		Download (1MB)		Not Available ⑦	
	Download (2.6GB) 10015 images and 1 ground truth response CSV file (containing 1 header row and 10015 corresponding response rows).				Download (40MB)	Not Available ⑦	
3		Download (3EKB)	Download (51MB)	Download (7KB)	1512 images.		CC-BY-NC
	Download (481KB) 10015 entries grouping each lesion by image and diagnosis confirm type.						

Figure 4- ISIC2018 test ground truth data not available

Melanoma is defined as a form of malignant skin cancer that is very threatening to health. It represents 1% of skin cancers but causes a large majority of skin cancer deaths [3]. Proper diagnosis of melanoma at an earlier stage is crucial for the success rate of complete cure. However, skin cancer is uncontrollable in terms of growth of its abnormal skin cells. This kind of tumor of the skin is the most common of all cancers; It occurs when DNA damage to skin cells, which are often caused by ultraviolet radiation from sunshine or tanning beds. It triggers mutations, or genetic defects, that lead the skin cells to mutate much rapidly and form malignant tumors.

Traditionally, skin cancer is diagnosed by physical examination and biopsy that is a quick and simple procedure where part or all of the spot is removed and sent to a laboratory. It may be done by the doctor or a dermatologist or surgeon. Nonetheless, results take about a week to come through. This manual diagnosis is time-consuming, expensive and may be wrong due to the bias of the dermatologist.

Most recently, dermoscopic images with forms of skin cancer could be analyzed by computer vision system to streamline the process of skin cancer detection. Therefore, we are able to see classification system surpasses human in big datasets like ImageNet [1]. Using Automated DL skin lesion classification is viable approach to deal with the diagnosis of melanoma.

3.5.1 Remarks of detecting a melanoma:

There are two important methods to detect a melanoma. These methods are important to understand the necessary features that would help either manual or automated ML or DL in detecting and classifying the 7 types of melanoma lesions. Three-point checklist ABB is a typical method for diagnosis of melanoma and skin lesion, which is provided in the following [2]:

- Asymmetry: symmetry of color and structure in one or two perpendicular axes

- Atypical network: pigment network with irregular holes and thick lines

- Blue-white structures: any type of blue and/or white color, for example, combination of blue-white veil and regression structures.

Additionally, ABCD parameters method is also common for diagnosis of melanoma [2]:

- Asymmetrical shape: melanoma lesions are typically asymmetrical.

- Borders: melanoma lesions have the irregular border.

- Color: the presence of more than one color in melanoma lesions.

- Diameter: melanoma lesions are typically larger than 6mm in diameter.

4. Approach

This section details firstly the pre-processing steps of data augmentation and split, secondly the parameters and settings of CNNs algorithm, and lastly the evaluation metrics that we would use to evaluate the 4 whole architectures.

4.1 Pre-processing

The pre-processing step includes the image resizing to 64x64, data augmentation by flipping, and lastly the data split to 75% training and 25% test sets.

4.1.1 Image Resizing

At first, it is important to specify the image size for the input of CNNs algorithm. So, we have adopted the 64x64 pixels by 3 channels because it has well proved competitive results. It is well experienced that the higher the pixels are, there would be a significant advancement in the results. However, we could have adopted higher resolutions but we had a problem with the shortness of memory capacity of 16GB, so 64x64 is well suited after much time of experiences. The following figure (5) shows a difference of the same image in different resolutions, so we could have a clearer view of the resizing problem. We could notice a huge different apparently in image resolution, for evidently the higher the pixels are, the image would contain higher information, so that it would advance the overall classification.

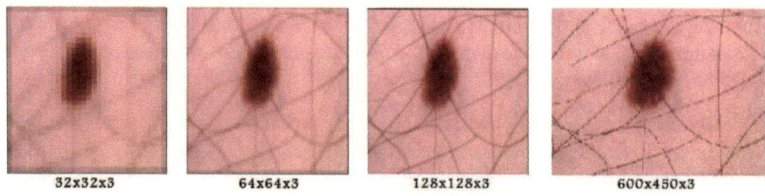

Figure 5- Different pixel versions of the same image in ISIC2018 dataset

4.1.2 Data augmentation

Training data are augmented from 10015 for 20030 after flipping each image in the opposite direction of its original. The following figure (6) demonstrates the original and its flipped version.

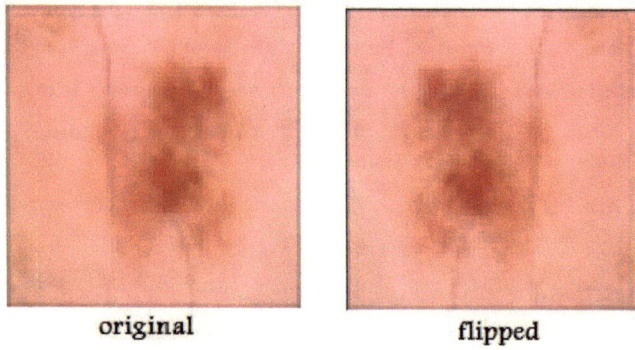

Figure 6- Original and its flipped version in the Final ISIC2018 dataset

4.1.2 Data split

The training data are split into two sets of training and testing sets. Firstly, the training set is 75% of the training dataset and the testing set is 25%. Therefore, the training set contains 15022 images and the testing set includes the rest of images that are 5008 pictures in total. Furthermore, the validation set contains 193 images, so they would be used to fine-tune the hyperparameters of the VGG16 architecture in training epoch by epoch.

4.2 Algorithm

With the existence of many deep CNNs models achieving competitive results in terms of the state-of-the art on ImageNet, I chose VGG16 to fine-tune the ISIC2018 dataset in our hands for its efficiency and simplicity. In this project, we have used VGG16 and not VGG16 nets, which is known as it contains 3 convolutional layers in its convolutional blocks [22]. The VGG16 schema is as specified in the following two figures (7) and (8).

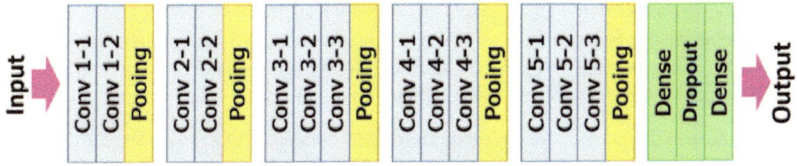

Figure 7- VGG16 Schema, edited from [22]

The input to VGG16 is a 224*224 RGB image. First of all, the pre-processing layer takes the RGB picture with its pixel values in range of 0 to 255 and subtracts the mean values. This computation is calculated over the entire ImageNet training set. After image pre-processing, input image is passed through a number of weighted convolutional layers. There are total of 13 convolutional layers and 2 fully connected layers in VGG16 architecture [24]. The architecture has small filters of 3x3 with deeper depth. In experiments, it has proved the same effective receptive field as having larger filters of, for example, 7x7 convolutional filters.

In addition, the architecture has same 5 maximum pooling layers. There consists of two fully connected layers (FCL), the first contains 512 channels which is followed by another FCL of 7 channels to predict 7 labels. The Last fully connected layer uses a softmax function for classifying the input image.

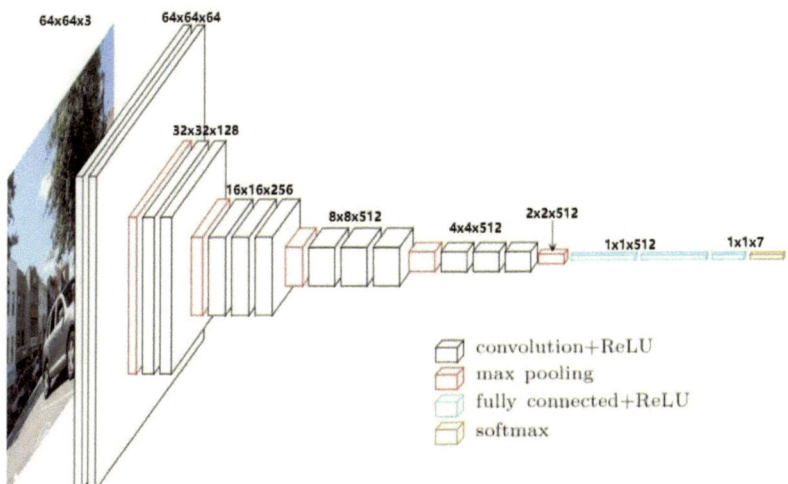

Figure 8- VGG16 detailed architecture, it contains 5 convolutional blocks, edited from [24]

The first two layers are convolutional layers with 3x3 filters with single stride. They use 64 filters that results in 64x64x64 volume. After the first two layers, pooling layer is used with max-pooling of 2x2 size and stride 2. Therefore, it reduces height and width of a volume from 64x64x64 to 32x32x128. Then, 2 more convolution layers with 128 filters are placed, which results a dimension of 32x32x128. After pooling layer is used, the volume is reduced to 16x16x256

Furthermore, two more convolution layers are added with 256 filters each followed by down sampling layer that reduces the size to 8x8x512. Next, two more 3 convolution stack layer is separated by a max-pooling layer. After the final pooling layer, 4x4x512 volume is flattened into FCL with 512 channels and the softmax function outputs one of the 7 classes.

For the purpose of this project, we have experimented 4 version of VGG16 architectures in fine-tuning the ISIC2018 dataset; therefore, we would explore the effectiveness of freezing different layers at each individual experiment. The fine-tuning is well preserving the pre-trained weights of VGG16 model on ImageNet. The four VGG16 settings are specified in the following subsections.

4.2.1 VGG16 LL (Last layer fine-tuning)
In this architecture, we have frozen the first four blocks of VGG16 and we have only left the last layer (the fifth block) to be fine-tuned on the ISIC2018 dataset.

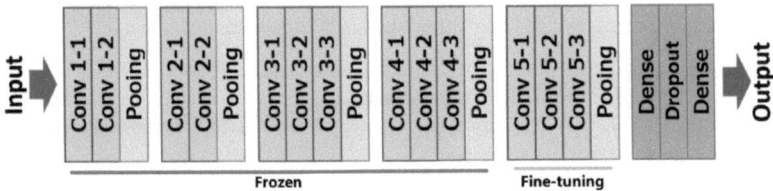

Figure 9- VGG16 last layer fine-tuning and freezing the rest of ConvNets

4.2.2 VGG16 FL (First layer fine-tuning)
In this architecture, we have frozen the last four blocks of VGG16 and we have only left the first layer (the first block) to be fine-tuned on the ISIC2018 dataset.

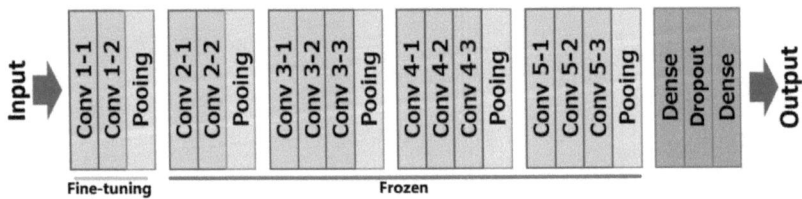

Figure 10- VGG16 first layer fine-tuning and freezing the rest of ConvNets

4.2.3 VGG16 ML (Middle layers fine-tuning)
In this architecture, we have frozen the first and last blocks of VGG16 and we have only left the middle layers (the second, third, and fourth blocks) to be fine-tuned on the ISIC2018 dataset.

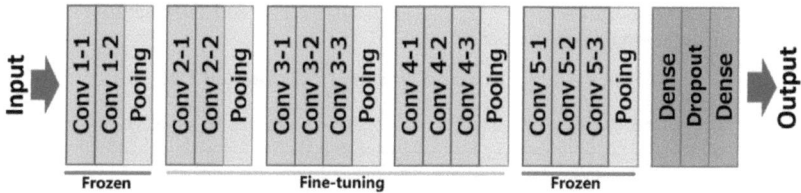

Figure 11- VGG16 middle layers fine-tuning and freezing the first and last layers of ConvNets

4.2.4 VGG16 FU (Full layers fine-tuning)

In this architecture, we have not frozen any of the ConvNets of VGG16 and we have fine-tuned the whole layers on the ISIC2018 dataset. The architecture as it is well visualized in figure (11), the models are initialized with the pre-trained weights on ImageNet.

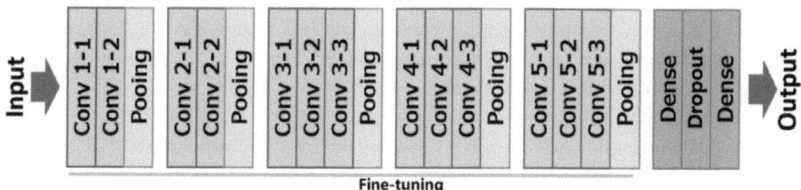

Figure 12- VGG16 full architecture fine-tuning

4.3 Evaluation Metrics

This section specifies the evaluation measures for assessing the performance of the different CNNs setting, which include accuracy, log loss (cross-entropy), and confusion matrix.

1) **Accuracy (A)**: Accuracy is mainly used to assess the whole efficiency of the classifier, but it is not a trust-worthy measure because it does specify the performance in terms of information relevance and predication. It is computed by diving the total number of correct classified points (true positives T_P and true negatives T_N) over the total number of points.

$$A = \frac{\#T_P + \#T_N}{\#total\ data\ points} \qquad (1)$$

2) **Log Loss (LL)**: Cross-entropy is a measure to assess the loss of function through the following computation:

$$LL = -\frac{1}{N}\sum_{i=1}^{N} y_i \cdot \log(p(y_i)) + (1 - y_i) \cdot \log(1 - p(y_i)), \qquad (2)$$

where y_i is the actual label of image i over N total ones. In our case, the labels are seven labels for the image types of skin lesions. Lastly, $p(y_i)$ is the predicated probability of the class by the DL model.

3) **Confusion matrix (CM)**: it is useful for describing the performance of classification tasks on test data with known true values. The matrix uses four main rates of true

positives (T_P), true negatives (T_N), false positives (F_P), and false negatives (F_N), as specified in the following table:

Table 3- Confusion Matrix in Binary Classification Task

Actual\Predicated	Predicted: Negative	Predicted: Positive
Actual: Negative	T_N	F_P
Actual: Positive	F_N	T_P

5. Experiments and Results

The architectures of VGG16 conducted in Keras framework for the availability of resources and the good documentation of use. Tables (4) and (5) compare the results obtained in implementing the different VGG16 architectures in consideration to state-of-the-art studies. Most effectively, the fourth model VGG16 FU outperformed the three proposed VGG16 architectures, which is well seen from the accuracy and loss reports. On one hand, it is well cited that VGG16 FU has achieved a 1.0 training accuracy and $5.15e^{-07}$ loss as well as 0.903 validation accuracy and 0.896 loss, and 0.9041 test accuracy and 0.893 loss. On the other hand, the rest of the architectures proved a well significance results as in VGG16 ML, which has achieved a 1.0 training accuracy and $5.69e^{-06}$ loss as well as 0.89 validation accuracy and 0.87 loss, and 0.898 test accuracy and 0.868 loss. The rest of evaluations of the two remaining architectures are provided in the following table (4):

Algorithm\Criteria	Training		Validation		Test	
	Loss	Accuracy	Loss	Accuracy	Loss	Accuracy
VGG16 LL	4.2830e-05	1.0000	0.9960	0.8646	0.9934	0.8646
VGG16 FL	3.0070e-05	1.0000	1.0118	0.8680	1.0094	0.8680
VGG16 ML	5.6995e-06	1.0000	0.8712	0.8988	0.8689	0.8989
VGG16 FU	5.1577e-07	1.0000	0.8968	0.9038	0.8939	0.9041

Table 4- The performance of the different VGG16 architectures on ISIC2018 dataset

However, the models have showed an overfitting problem that is well manifested in the loss and accuracy reports. It is well noticed that as the training accuracy goes higher, the validation remains still steady without a slight change and that problem would damage the generality of the models. Nonetheless, the fine-tuning of the whole architecture as it is well proven in VGG16 FU has surpassed the problem in updating and training all parameters on the ISIC2018 dataset. It is still there a remaining promise in using other competitive architectures as ResNet and InceptionNet.

Table 5- The results of the different VGG16 models in accuracy and loss metrices

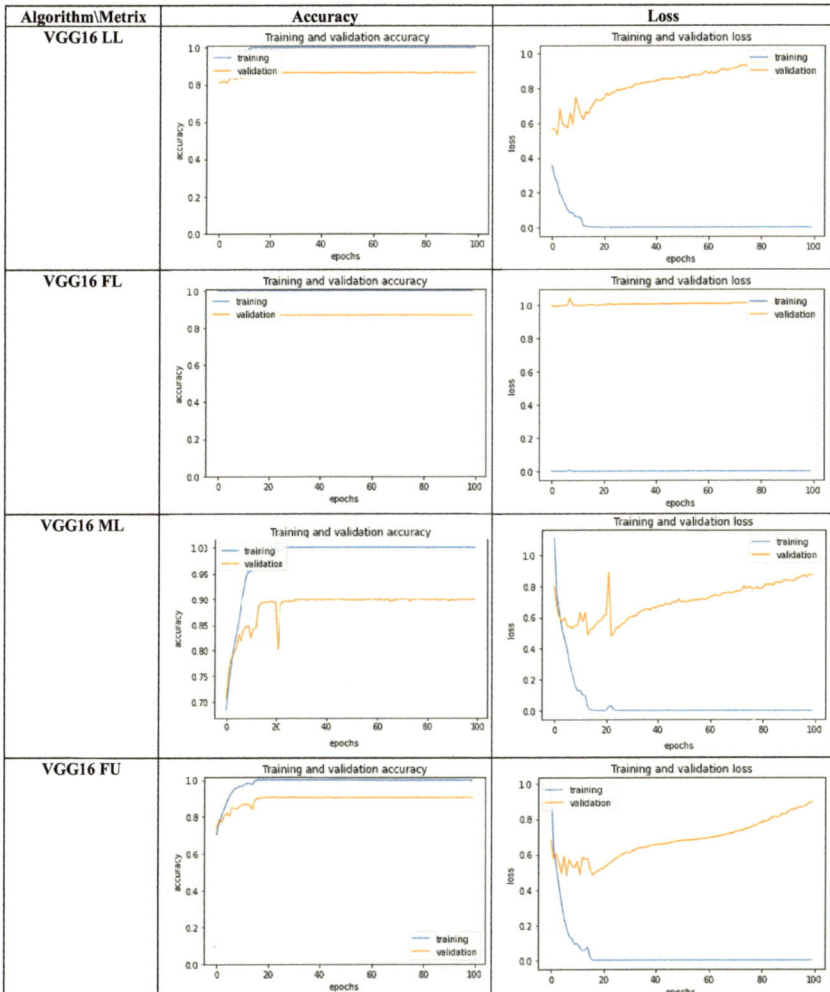

All the four experiments on ISIC2018 dataset have been trained on the training set with THE validation set to measure the performance of the architectures in each epoch. The training epochs fixed for 100; therefore, a clear optimal accuracy obtained for training convergence. Besides, we have noted a small batch size of training for better iteration update using Adam optimizer. In addition to the results obtained on each architecture, learning rate (LR) is initialized at 0.01 and Adam optimizer is used to update the parameters. LR decay is also used

CNNs for Medical Images Classification

so that the LR will halve whenever the validation accuracy plateaus for 3 epochs. This technique is employed for its great help in increasing the algorithm optimization and generalization.

Furthermore, there are huge similarity in the detailed results obtained through the CM. As we could see in the below table (6), the same amount of concentration is repeated in all the architectures and that is well obvious from the same representation colors. For example, classification class number 1 is sharing the same amount of correction in all the architectures as it is colored white cream. The same applies to all other classes. However, we could notice a huge misprediction that is well concentrated in specific classes like between 1 and 4 as well as 0 and 4. The same errors are committed in all the four experiments of VGG16. So, it is a matter of further investigation in comparison with other models and DL hyper-parameters tuning.

Table 6- The results of the different VGG16 models in respect to Confusion Metrix

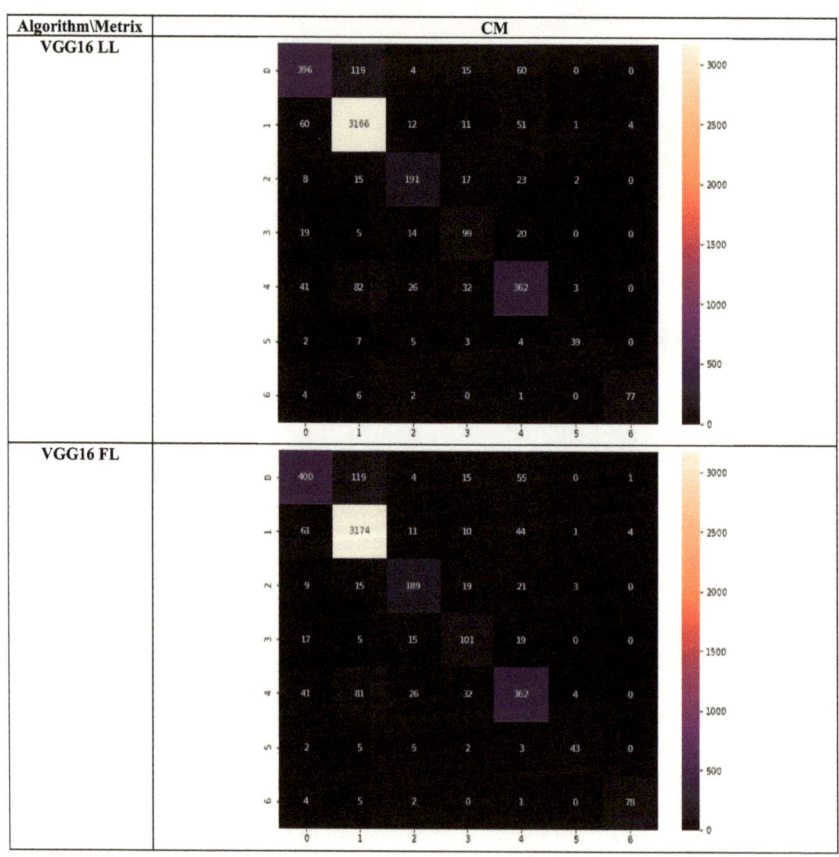

Algorithm\Metrix	CM
VGG16 ML	
VGG16 FU	

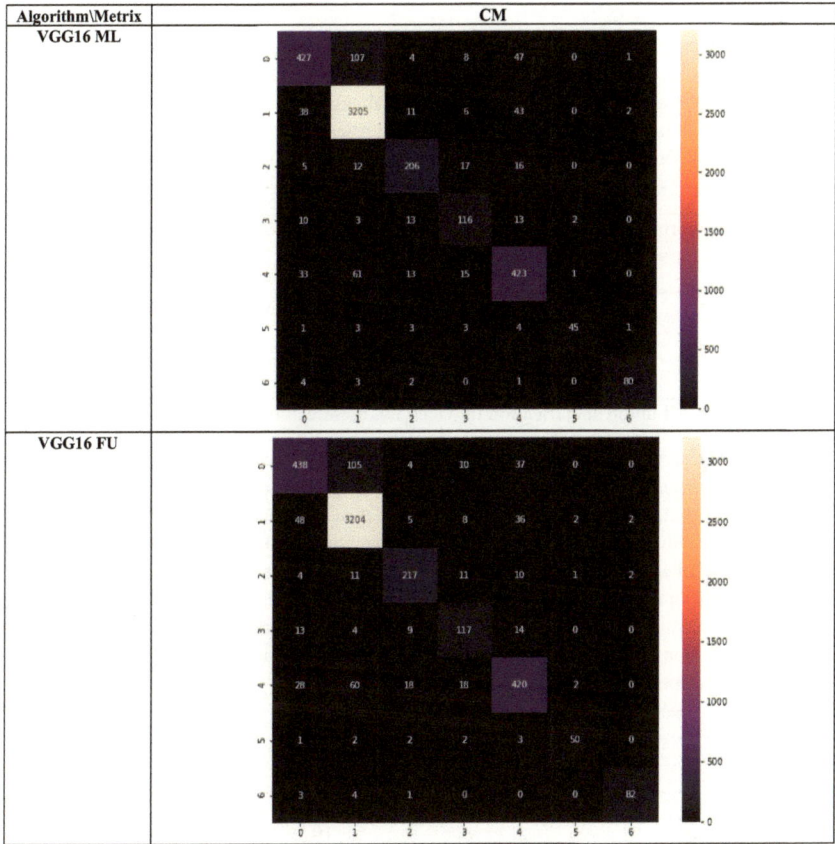

6. Conclusion

By the art of transfer learning and deep learning, I was able to experiment different settings of VGG16 on ISIC2018 dataset and the best model VGG16 FU achieved a total accuracy of 90% on validation set and 90% on test set. Through experiments, I have also found that for this dataset, fine-tuning the whole model not only gives better end result but also helps the model converges much faster than fine-tuning the rest of the layers. One serious problem observed during training is overfitting. All of my experiments overfit the training data for a large percentage after approximal the 20th epoch, as we could observe the loss of the validation set goes higher and training loss goes lower. Many methods are used to minimize overfitting, but I wasn't able to narrow down the amount of overfit further.

6.1 Future Works

Future work would be considered in avoiding overfitting as well as better training strategy will be adapted to help the models in reaching convergence. Furthermore, including more data would be prioritized for boosting the models in better feature learning and prediction.

6.2 Challenges

I have faced many difficulties in terms of setting up the Anaconda environment, which was totally not suitable for starting up the proposed CNNs algorithm. Also, the limited computational resources are the most difficult challenge because I could not upgrade my personal laptop to improve the whole results of the research project. The following table (7) specifies the specifications of the laptop that we have tested the four VGG16 architectures on.

Name	MSI GL75 Leopard 10SER
Central processor unit	Intel Core i7-10750H processor (Hexa-Core 2.6 GHz/5 GHz Turbo - 12 Threads - Cache 12M)
RAM	16 GB of 2666 MHz DDR4 RAM (2x8 GB)
Graphic card	NVIDIA GeForce RTX 2060 graphics chip with 6 GB of dedicated GDDR6 memory

Table 7- Laptop specification in which DL architectures trained and tested

Unfortunately, I have not had an access to the supports of the XLIM laboratory, though it would have been a great pushup. Also, it is a challenging experience to go through different algorithms in independent soul, but also for testing the most out of the state-of-the-art approaches. It is well persisted challenge to go through all the mathematical background of DL as the time is really a glimpse of an eye. Lastly, the timing of the experiments is considered highly expensive in terms of fully consumption of computational power in low speed of evaluations; I have had been restricted to time, awaiting the architectures to finish up training. Therefore, I could apply further modifications and improvements. The total hours of training and testing the four VGG16 architectures are specified in the following table:

Algorithm	Time in Hours
VGG16 LL	13
VGG16 FL	6
VGG16 ML	14
VGG16 FU	19

Table 8- Approximate time consumption in training and testing the four VGG16 architectures

References

[1] Deng, J., Dong, W., Socher, R., Li, L.-J., Li, K., & Fei-Fei, L. (2009). Imagenet: A large-scale hierarchical image database. In 2009 IEEE conference on computer vision and pattern recognition (pp. 248–255).

[2] Peris, K., Zalaudek, I., Argenziano, G., Soyer, H., Corona, R., Sera, F., Blum, A., Braun, R., Cabo, H., Ferrara, G., Kopf, A., Langford, D., Menzies, S., Pellacani, G., & Seidenari, S. (2006). Three-point checklist of dermoscopy: an open internet study. British Journal of Dermatology, 154, 431-437. https://doi.org/10.1111/j.1365-2133.2005.06983.x

[3] Melanoma Skin Cancer Statistics. (2021). Retrieved April 28, 2021, from https://www.cancer.org/cancer/melanoma-skin-cancer/about/key-statistics.html

[4] Yap, J., Nozdryn-Plotnicki, A., & Yolland, W. (2018). ISIC Meetup Presentation. Retrieved April 28, 2021, from https://docs.google.com/presentation/d/1Lup8MnuOkVakDL5-VWx14n-94pEKRq6cY88xoO6MF0w/edit#slide=id.p1

[5] Barata, C., Celebi, M. E., & Marques, J. S. (2015). Improving dermoscopy image classification using color constancy. IEEE journal of biomedical and health informatics, 19(3), 1146–1152. https://doi.org/10.1109/JBHI.2014.2336473

[6] Lin, T., Goyal, P., Girshick, R.B., He, K., & Dollár, P. (2017). Focal Loss for Dense Object Detection. 2017 IEEE International Conference on Computer Vision (ICCV), 2999-3007.

[7] Hu, J., Shen, L., & Sun, G. (2018). Squeeze-and-Excitation Networks. 2018 IEEE/CVF Conference on Computer Vision and Pattern Recognition, 7132-7141.

[8] Carcagnì, P., Cuna, A., & Distante, C. (2018). A Dense CNN approach for skin lesion classification. ArXiv, abs/1807.06416.

[9] Milton, M.A. (2019). Automated Skin Lesion Classification Using Ensemble of Deep Neural Networks in ISIC 2018: Skin Lesion Analysis Towards Melanoma Detection Challenge. ArXiv, abs/1901.10802.

[10] Guissous, A.E. (2019). Skin Lesion Classification Using Deep Neural Network. ArXiv, abs/1911.07817.

[11] Mahbod, A., Schaefer, G., Wang, C., Ecker, R., Dorffner, G., & Ellinger, I. (2020). Investigating and Exploiting Image Resolution for Transfer Learning-based Skin Lesion Classification. ArXiv, abs/2006.14715.

[12] Yao, P., Shen, S., Xu, M., Liu, P., Zhang, F., Xing, J., Shao, P., Kaffenberger, B., & Xu, R. (2021). Single Model Deep Learning on Imbalanced Small Datasets for Skin Lesion Classification. ArXiv, abs/2102.01284.

[13] Masson, J. (2018). Lintelligence artificielle: Rêve ou cauchemar: Séminaire, juin 2018. Retrieved May 3, 2021, from https://www.fnmr.org/publication/autres/pdf/201811_fnmr_livre_ia_english.pdf

[14] Standford University. (2017). RSNA 2017: Rads who use AI will replace rads who don't. Retrieved May 3, 2021, from https://aimi.stanford.edu/news/rsna-2017-rads-who-use-ai-will-replace-rads-who-don-t

[15] Meskó, B., Görög, M. (2020). A short guide for medical professionals in the era of artificial intelligence. npj Digit. Med. 3, 126. https://doi.org/10.1038/s41746-020-00333-z

[16] ECR 2019: Book of Abstracts. (2019). Insights Imaging 10, 22. https://doi.org/10.1186/s13244-019-0713-y

[17]   A. Krizhevsky, I. Sutskever, and G. E. Hinton. (2012). Imagenet classification with deep convolutional neural networks. In Advances in neural information processing systems, pages1097–1105.

[18]   K. He, X. Zhang, S. Ren, and J. Sun. (2015). Deep residual learning for image recognition. arXiv preprint arXiv:1512.03385.

[19]   Wood, T. (2019). Convolutional Neural Network. Retrieved May 3, 2021, from https://deepai.org/machine-learning-glossary-and-terms/convolutional-neural-network

[20]   Raghu, M., Zhang, C., Kleinberg, J., & Bengio, S. (2019). Transfusion: Understanding transfer learning for medical imaging. In Advances in neural information processing systems (pp. 3347-3357).

[21]   Xlim   Présentation.   (n.d.).   Retrieved   May   10,   2021,   from https://www.xlim.fr/laboratoire/presentation

[22]   Ul Hassan, M. (2021, February 24). VGG16 - Convolutional Network for Classification and Detection. Retrieved May 20, 2021, from https://neurohive.io/en/popular-networks/vgg16/

[23]   LeCun, Y., Bottou, L., Bengio, Y., & Haffner, P. (1998). Gradient-based learning applied to document recognition.

[24]   Frossard, D. (2016, June 17). VGG in TensorFlow. Retrieved May 22, 2021, from https://www.cs.toronto.edu/~frossard/post/vgg16